A GUIDE TO STORYTELLING

HOW TO TELL A FABLE

Suri Rosen

www.av2books.com

Step 1
Go to **www.av2books.com**

Step 2
Enter this unique code
ANVWO30IY

Step 3
Explore your interactive eBook!

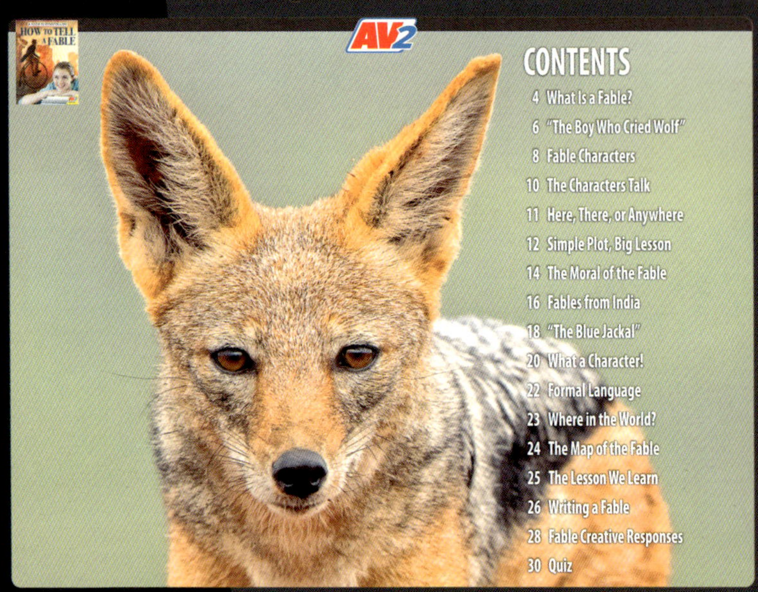

AV2 is optimized for use on any device

Your interactive eBook comes with...

Contents
Browse a live contents page to easily navigate through resources

Audio
Listen to sections of the book read aloud

Videos
Watch informative video clips

Weblinks
Gain additional information for research

Try This!
Complete activities and hands-on experiments

Key Words
Study vocabulary, and complete a matching word activity

Quizzes
Test your knowledge

Slideshows
View images and captions

... and much, much more!

Contents

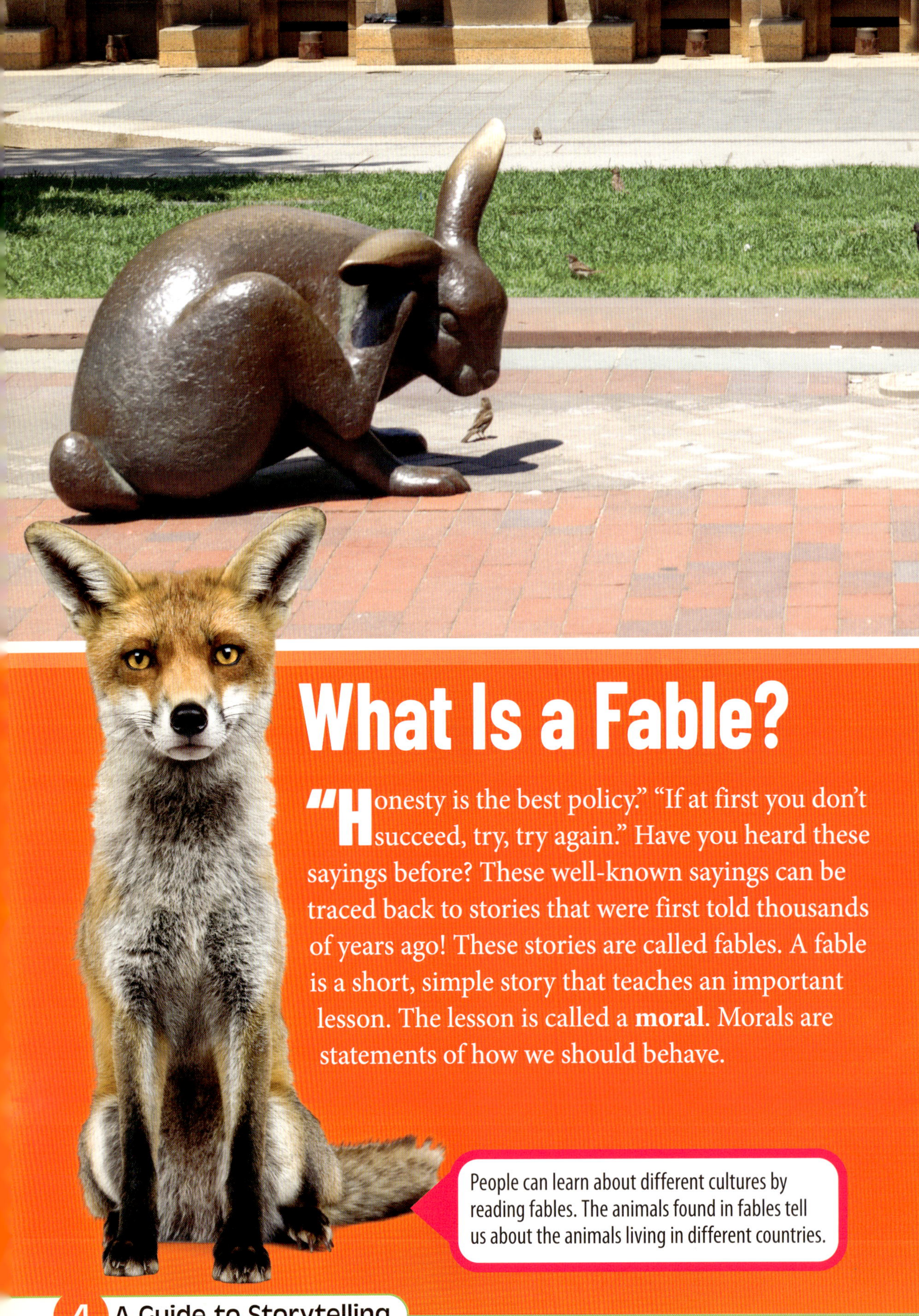

What Is a Fable?

"Honesty is the best policy." "If at first you don't succeed, try, try again." Have you heard these sayings before? These well-known sayings can be traced back to stories that were first told thousands of years ago! These stories are called fables. A fable is a short, simple story that teaches an important lesson. The lesson is called a **moral**. Morals are statements of how we should behave.

People can learn about different cultures by reading fables. The animals found in fables tell us about the animals living in different countries.

Fables have been told for thousands of years. People told fables to entertain listeners and teach them at the same time. Fables are tales that show us how being wise and making good choices are always rewarded.

Behaving badly will always get a **character** into trouble in a fable. Fables offer lessons about life and ourselves. They show us how we should behave.

Write Your Own Fable

1 Prewriting

Think of a fable you might want to write. Follow each step as you read through this book to help create a fable of your own.

Because the purpose of a fable is to teach a lesson, start with the lesson you want to teach. Think of something that is important for people to know. Here is a list to get you started:

- Do not put off until tomorrow what you can do today.
- Look before you leap.
- Do what you know how to do best.

The Boy Who Cried Wolf

There once was a young **shepherd** who watched over a flock of sheep just outside his small village. Every morning, the boy led the sheep up a small hill to a pasture and watched over them as the flock nibbled the grass.

The boy spent his days alone with the sheep. He had no one to talk to or play with. Every day, he grew more bored. The minutes began to feel like hours.

One day, the boy had an idea. He decided to pretend that a wolf had come to hurt the sheep.

The boy stood on the hill and faced the village below. He yelled as loudly as he could, "Wolf! Wolf! The wolf is chasing the sheep!"

The men from the village ran up the hill to help the boy. They looked around but saw no wolf. "Where is the wolf?" they asked.

The boy burst into laughter. "I was just pretending," he said, laughing. What a wonderful way to break up a boring afternoon!

The men stared at the grinning boy. "That is not funny!" said the men. They turned and stomped back down the hill to the village.

The next day, the boy sat alone on the hill watching the sheep. Once again he grew bored. It had been so exciting when the men came running when he called. He wanted to have a bit more fun.

The boy stood on the hill and faced the village below. He yelled as loudly as he could, "Wolf! Wolf! The wolf is chasing the sheep!"

The men from the village again raced up the hill. "Where is the wolf?" they asked as they scanned the pasture.

The boy burst out laughing again. It was so easy to fool these simple people.

"There is no wolf," answered the boy. "It was just a joke."

"How dare you waste our time," said one man, loudly. "Call us only when there is real trouble!" He turned and stomped back to the village. The other men followed him in angry silence.

The next day, the boy lay on the grass and felt the warm sun on his face. The sheep began to bleat loudly. The boy sat up.

In the distance, the boy saw a wolf coming. The boy's heart began to race.

He cried out, "Wolf! There's a wolf in the pasture! Please! Someone come right away. The sheep are scared!"

The wolf inched closer. The sheep suddenly ran off in different directions.

"Wooolf," the boy yelled. "He is getting closer!" The boy ran to the edge of the hill and looked at the village below. He could see the people in the village going on with their day. Nobody was listening to his calls for help.

The boy picked up a rock. His hands shook as the wolf came closer. He raised his hand and threw the rock at the wolf. It hit the wolf's leg. The wolf growled. It turned and limped back into the forest.

The sheep were now spread out over the hill. The boy spent the rest of the afternoon rounding them up without any help from anyone.

Fable Characters

Characters in fables are different from characters in other kinds of stories. Characters in fables can be people, animals, or other creatures. The characters are very simple. We usually know very little about them. A character in a fable has one main trait. A trait is a part of a character's personality. We learn about characters and their traits by what they do. Read the two passages below.

Once again he grew bored. It had been so exciting when the men came running when he called. He wanted to have a bit more fun.

The boy burst out laughing again. It was so easy to fool these simple people.

Shepherding is one of the oldest jobs on the planet. People have been doing it for about 5,000 years.

We do not know much about the boy. We do understand something important, though. The boy likes to tell lies as a joke. He laughs at the men for running to help him. He does not care that fooling the men will waste their time.

Certain animals are related to specific traits. Sheep are often depicted as shy and fearful.

We do not know much about the village men who answer the boy's cries for help. They are hard workers, but they are willing to stop work and come to help him. They all trust the boy and believe him when he asks for their help. They act responsibly.

Write Your Own Fable

2 Explore a Character

Choose a character that will be at the center of your fable. Give your character one strong trait. Your character may be foolish or wise, carefree or serious. Will this trait get the character into trouble?

The Characters Talk

When characters speak, it is called **dialogue**. Quotation marks (“ ”) are always placed around a character’s exact words. Dialogue makes characters seem like real people and helps the story come alive. We can learn much about people by what they say and how they say it.

“How dare you waste our time,” said one man, loudly. “Call us only when there is real trouble!”

The man’s words are angry, and he speaks loudly. This helps you picture him in your mind.

Dialogue also moves a story forward. Every time the boy yells wolf, something happens. The men come running in the beginning because they trust the boy. Then, they stop believing him when he keeps lying.

Write Your Own Fable

3 Explore the Problem

Put your character together with a problem. Write a sentence about the character and the problem.

- A carefree grasshopper plays all day instead of working.
- A foolish monkey tries to be as strong as an elephant.

Here, There, or Anywhere

The **setting** is the *place* where the story happens. Fables do not really give much detail about the setting. They often take place in places that could be almost anywhere in the world. There are just enough details to help us understand the action.

The setting is also the *time* period when the story takes place. Fables take place sometime in the past, because these stories were created many, many years ago. "The Boy Who Cried Wolf" is one of the most famous fables written by Aesop, the ancient Greek storyteller. This fable is still repeated all over the world because it still has a lesson to teach us.

Very little is known about Aesop. Some people believe he may have been a Greek slave.

Think About It!

Does it matter what country or culture this fable comes from? Do we need to know that it comes from ancient Greece? Why or why not?

Simple Plot, Big Lesson

The **plot** is what happens in a story. A fable has a simple plot. It starts with a single problem that the main character must solve. The problem is also called a **conflict**. The events are all about how the problem gets solved.

The **climax** is the moment of greatest excitement. In a fable, it is often the moment when the main character realizes something. It usually comes close to the end of the fable. The ending wraps up the story. It is called the **resolution**.

The plots of fables often include **repetition**. This builds the humor as well as the suspense. In the fable "The Three Little Pigs," each pig builds a house. One builds his house out of straw. One builds his house out of sticks. The third builds his house out of bricks. The action and dialogue are repeated two times. The third time, the result is different. Here is an example of repetition from the fable "The Three Little Pigs."

The wolf came to the house made of straw. "Let me in, let me in," said the wolf. "Or I'll huff and I'll puff and I'll blow your house in!"

"Not by the hair of my chinny chin chin!" cried the little pig. So the wolf huffed and he puffed and he blew the house in.

The wolf came to the house made of sticks. "Let me in, let me in," said the wolf. "Or I'll huff and I'll puff and I'll blow your house in!"

"Not by the hair of my chinny chin chin!" cried the little pig. So the wolf huffed and he puffed and he blew the house in.

Repetition helps us predict the ending. How do you think the fable of the three little pigs ends?

Story Map for "The Boy Who Cried Wolf"

A **story map** shows the basic parts of a plot.

Characters
boy, villagers

Setting
a pasture, a long time ago

Problem
The boy is bored.

Events

1. The bored boy watches sheep.
2. The boy pretends there is a wolf and calls for help.
3. The men come to save the sheep.
4. The boy cries wolf again and the men return.
5. Climax: The boy calls out for help but the men do not come this time.

Resolution
The boy must fight the wolf and gather the sheep on his own.

Lesson
The boy learns that nobody believes a liar, even when he tells the truth.

The Moral of the Fable

The plot is what the fable is about. A **theme** is the message of the fable. Fables always teach us important life lessons. These lessons are also called morals. A fable entertains us with a good story. The moral gives us words to live by. The whole purpose of the fable is to teach this lesson.

Sometimes, the moral is stated at the end of the fable. Sometimes, we have to think about the fable and find the lesson ourselves. We see what the lesson means because the moral is expressed very clearly through the actions and events in the fable.

The lessons learned from reading fables can stay with people for a long time.

Think About It!

Moral: Nobody believes a liar, even when he tells the truth.

- What does this moral teach us?
- What might happen if we tell lies?
- How should we behave?

A fable can change the ways that people talk and write. Today, when people raise false alarms, they are often said to be "crying wolf."

Write Your Own Fable

4 The Main Events

Use a story map to plan the events in your story. Keep the lesson in mind as you write your events. Include only key events in your fable. Remember, fables are short!

Fables from India

One important group of fables is called the *Panchatantra*. This is a collection of ancient Indian fables that were compiled in the 3rd century BC. These stories were based on fables that had been around for thousands of years. The *Panchatantra* fables are also filled with animals, creatures, and spirits. All of them talk and behave like people.

"The Elephants and the Hares" is a *Panchatantra* fable that tells the story of a group of hares that lose their home to a herd of elephants. It shows how the weak can overcome the mighty.

The *Panchatantra* fable "The Blue **Jackal**" is a lot like "The Boy Who Cried Wolf." The main character—the jackal—is very clever. Like the boy who cried wolf, the jackal fools the other characters. Both fables start with a main character who has a problem. The problem causes some interesting events. At the end of the fable, the moral becomes clear. As in every fable, the main character always gets what he deserves!

Write Your Own Fable

5 Write a First Draft

Put all your ideas down on paper. Do not worry about getting everything right. This is just a first draft to get you started. Use a pencil and write lightly so that you can erase your mistakes when you revise.

Fable Checklist:

- Do I have a character with a strong trait?
- Does the character want something?
- Do the events focus on the problem?
- Does my fable end with a moral?

The Blue Jackal

There once was a jackal named Fierce-Howl. He lived alone in a cave at the edge of a town. He was always hungry and was forever looking for food. One night, his empty stomach hurt so much that he had to do something. Fierce-Howl wandered into the town to search for food. He found a heap of garbage and began sniffing and scratching it. He hoped he would find something to eat.

A pack of dogs heard his sounds and surrounded him. The dogs growled and barked. Terrified, Fierce-Howl turned away from the pack. He fled from the garbage heap and raced through the town. The dogs chased him, barking and biting him along the way.

Fierce-Howl did not know where to go. He bolted through the streets with the dogs on his heels. His heart pounded with fear. He looked for hiding places but could not find any.

The jackal suddenly spotted an open door to a house. Finally, he thought, I am safe! He jumped through the doorway and landed in a big pot of blue dye! He climbed out of the pot. His fur was completely blue. Somehow, he escaped from the town and returned to the forest.

When he arrived in the forest, the other animals spotted him right away. What was this strange blue creature? No one had ever seen anything like it. They fled in terror away from Fierce-Howl.

"Why do you run away?" he called out to them.

But then Fierce-Howl had an idea. "I am king of all of the creatures of the forest," he said to the other animals.

The lions, tigers, leopards, monkeys, and rabbits bowed before him. "How may we serve you?" they asked.

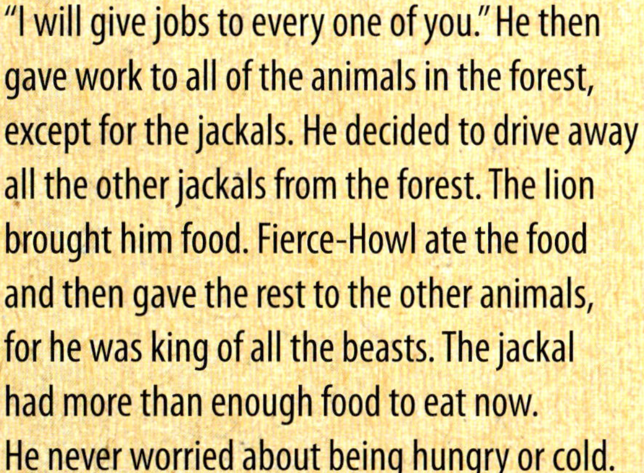

"I will give jobs to every one of you." He then gave work to all of the animals in the forest, except for the jackals. He decided to drive away all the other jackals from the forest. The lion brought him food. Fierce-Howl ate the food and then gave the rest to the other animals, for he was king of all the beasts. The jackal had more than enough food to eat now. He never worried about being hungry or cold.

One night, he sat in his court and heard a sound. A pack of jackals howled together. Fierce-Howl's eyes filled with tears of happiness. It had been so long since he had been with his own kind. The howling was like music. He remembered how much he missed sharing his life with the pack. He could not help himself. He jumped to his feet and howled along with jackals in the forest.

The lions and the other animals heard Fierce-Howl howling with the jackals. When they heard his howling, they realized that he was not really a king. He was just a jackal! He had lied to them. At first, they were ashamed. He had fooled them. They had believed that he was their king. But then they grew angry. They found Fierce-Howl and chased him. Fierce-Howl fled from the forest and was never able to return.

What a Character!

The main character in this fable is Fierce-Howl, the jackal. Even though he is an animal, he talks and acts like a person. We know very little about him. We see a bit about what he is like by the way he acts as the story moves forward.

At the start of the fable, he is hungry. As the story continues, we see other parts of his character. He is scared when the dogs chase him. When he enters the forest, he thinks of a good lie. He is clever. Finally, when he hears the other jackals howling, we see that he is lonely.

At the end of the fable, the jackal has been chased from his home in the forest. He is once again just a jackal, not a strange animal that is a king. But we hope that he has learned an important lesson! Do you think the jackal is wise at the end?

Write Your Own Fable

6 Revise Your Fable

Reread your fable. Now is your chance to change it and make it even better.

- Does the plot make sense?
- Would adding another event make the fable clearer?
- Does it have a lesson or moral?

Jackals are native to Africa, Asia, and southeastern Europe.

Formal Language

Dialogue helps bring the characters to life. We see from the dialogue that the jackal decides to act like a powerful animal. The animals in the forest accept that he is their king.

The lions, tigers, leopards, monkeys, and rabbits bowed before him. "How may we serve you?" they asked.

Listening to stories read aloud helps children hear the differences between formal and casual language.

The dialogue in this fable is formal. The characters do not speak the way people speak in conversation. The formal language makes the fable more important. People use formal language when they want us to remember their words. Storytellers tell fables to help us learn. We pay more attention to the lesson because of the language.

Write Your Own Fable

7 Proofread Your Draft

Check carefully for any spelling mistakes or poor grammar. Use the proofreading checklist below to help you.

- Did I indent all paragraphs?
- Did I use capital letters for proper nouns?
- Did I spell each word correctly?
- Did I punctuate dialogue correctly?

Where in the World?

"The Blue Jackal" is a fable from India. There are only a few details about where the story is set in this fable. We do know that the jackal lives in a cave in a forest. We also know the forest is close to a town. That is normal for fables. The setting in a fable could be taking place in any country at almost any time in the past.

Fables are timeless. Their lessons can be applied to any time, place, and situation. The house in the town is very important to the fable. This is where the jackal jumps into blue dye. The forest is important, too. This is where the jackal lives among the other animals. That is all we really need to know about where the story takes place.

Caves are common around the world. They can be found on each of Earth's continents.

Think About It!

Is the setting in this fable like the one in "The Boy Who Cried Wolf"? How are they different?

The Map of the Fable

The plot is what happens in the story. The jackal's problem—hunger—drives the action. Each event leads to another event. The jackal thinks he has solved the problem, but his dishonesty leads to his punishment.

The turning point, or climax, comes when the jackal hears the other jackals and starts to howl. The other animals suddenly realize that their king is really just a blue jackal. The resolution comes quickly.

Jackals are popular characters in fables around the world. They are often represented as tricksters.

Story Map for "The Blue Jackal"

Characters
the jackal and other forest animals

Setting
a forest and a town

Resolution
The animals chase the jackal out of the forest. He is not allowed to return to the forest.

Lesson
It is always better to be yourself instead of pretending to be someone else.

The Lesson We Learn

The jackal goes from hunger and danger to becoming king of the forest. Yet, the fable does not end on this happy note.

These events contain the lesson of this fable. The moral here is that it does not pay to pretend to be someone you are not. The jackal cannot escape who he really is. Now he must leave his home.

Write Your Own Fable

8 Make a Final Copy

Neatly copy your fable onto clean paper. Add a title to your fable. If you like, you can write it in colored markers. You can also draw some pictures to show what is happening in your fable. Think of some other ways to share your fable.

Problem

The jackal is hungry.

Events

1. The jackal goes to town to search for food.
2. A pack of dogs chase him.
3. While trying to escape the dogs, the jackal enters a house and falls into a pot of blue dye.
4. The jackal tells the other animals that he is king of all creatures.
5. Climax: The jackal howls and the other animals discover he is a jackal, not a king.

Writing a Fable

Writing a fable may take several tries. It is important to look over each draft of a story you write. You may find things that are wrong or that you wish to change.

Abdul chose a lesson that he wanted people to learn. His main character is a foolish monkey who wants to keep a fox from stealing his food. He thinks he can solve the problem by becoming as big as an elephant. Here is his first draft. It has some mistakes in it.

First Draft

Once there was a monkey and a fox. The fox always stole his food. The monkey wished that he could be as big as an elephant. That way he would be so strong that the fox would never dare take his food.

So the monkey started eating elephant food. He ate cabbage, lettuce, and grass. He ate all day long so he could have as much as an elephant would eat. But his stomach hurt him so much he couldn't do anything. His stomach hurt and he couldn't climb any more. The fox found him lying on the ground weak and in pain.

"Foolish animal," said the fox to the monkey. "Not only can you never become a different animal, you can't even be your own animal any more".

Dialogue Tips and Tricks

- Use quotation marks (" ") around a character's exact words.
- Use a comma to set off a person's exact words.
  "I eat lettuce," said the elephant.
- Begin the first word of a quotation with a capital letter and put an end mark before the last quotation mark.
  The monkey asked, "What do you eat, elephant?"

Abdul revised his first draft. He made his beginning stronger. He made changes to show how foolish the monkey was.

Second Draft

A monkey was mad because the fox always stole his seeds, nuts, and bananas. One day he complained about this to the elephant.

"Elephant," said the monkey, "I wish I could be huge and strong like you. What do you eat?"

"I eat cabbage, lettuce, and bananas," the elephant answered. "Hundreds of pounds every day."

The monkey decided to eat hundreds of pounds of elephant food all day. Then he would be as big and strong as an elephant. He ate all day. He grew big but he did not grow strong. He just grew big and round. One morning, the monkey was so big he couldn't even roll over.

The fox found the monkey lying on the ground in pain. The monkey hurt so much that he could not even move.

"Foolish monkey!" said the fox. "You can never become a different animal!"

Fable Creative Responses

Now you know what a fable is. Use what you learned to have fun with these creative activities. Share them with friends and classmates and compare your creations.

A News Report

Pretend that you are a reporter. You are telling TV viewers about the events in a fable. Imagine that you are at the fable's setting. Perform a live report. Interview some of the people or animals in the story. Ask them to tell their thoughts about the events.

Funny Fables!

Turn a fable into a comic book. Draw a picture of the fable's setting in your first box, and add a title. In each box after that, include pictures of the main events. In your last box, draw the resolution. Make sure that the boxes follow the order of the story!

Make a Board Game

Choose a fable that you like and list all of its events. Then, draw a game board on poster board. Draw one square for each event. If you like, you can add a drawing to each square. Add a few squares in between each event to make the game board longer. Your game board should have at least 20 squares. Label one end "Start" and one end "Moral." Cut out small pictures of some of the characters from the fable to use as markers. Roll the dice. If you land on an even number, you move ahead. If you land on an odd number, you have to go back to "Start." The first player to reach the end of the game yells, "I got plot!" and wins.

The Theme Queen

The Theme Queen is a talk-show host. She would like to interview you about a fable. She seems very surprised by the main character in the fable. Explain to her what the character did. Tell what important lesson the character learned, and explain the moral of the story.

Quiz

1 What does a fable help the reader understand?

2 What punctuation is placed around a character's exact words?

3 What two elements make up a story's setting?

4 What is the purpose of a story map?

5 What group of fables originated in India?

6 When do people use formal language?

7 What is the first step in writing a fable?

8 Who was Aesop?

ANSWERS: **1** Human behavior **2** Quotation marks **3** Place and time **4** To show the basic parts of a plot **5** The *Panchatantra* **6** On important occasions **7** Prewriting **8** An ancient Greek storyteller

Key Words

character: a person, animal, or creature in a story

climax: the peak of a story

conflict: a problem that the main character has to solve; a problem that causes trouble

dialogue: the words that a character speaks

jackal: a small animal that is related to wolves, dogs, and coyotes

moral: a life lesson taught in a fable

plot: the chain of events in a story

repetition: the repeating of actions or words for emphasis

resolution: the end of the story, when the plot's main problem is solved

setting: the time and place in which a story takes place

shepherd: someone who watches over sheep all day

story map: a diagram that shows the basic parts of the plot

theme: the main idea or lesson in a story

Index

Get the best of both worlds.

AV2 bridges the gap between print and digital.

The expandable resources toolbar enables quick access to content including **videos**, **audio**, **activities**, **weblinks**, **slideshows**, **quizzes**, and **key words**.

Animated videos make static images come alive.

Resource icons on each page help readers to further **explore key concepts**.

Published by AV2
14 Penn Plaza, 9th Floor
New York, NY 10122
Website: www.av2books.com

Library of Congress Control Number: 2020935555

ISBN 978-1-7911-3142-5 (hardcover)
ISBN 978-1-7911-3143-2 (softcover)
ISBN 978-1-7911-3138-8 (multi-user eBook)
ISBN 978-1-7911-3144-9 (single-user eBook)

Printed in Guangzhou, China
1 2 3 4 5 6 7 8 9 0 24 23 22 21 20

072020
101319

Project Coordinator: John Willis
Designer: Ana María Vidal

Photo Credits
Every reasonable effort has been made to trace ownership and to obtain permission to reprint copyright material. The publisher would be pleased to have any errors or omissions brought to its attention so that they may be corrected in subsequent printings. AV2 acknowledges Getty Images, Alamy, iStock, and Shutterstock as its primary image suppliers for this title.

First published by Crabtree Publishing Company in 2012.